*THE ALL NEW STYLE OF MAGAZINE-BOOKS*

**SDM**

www.SDMLIVE.com

**MP**

MOCY PUBLISHING
WWW.MOCYPUBLISHING.COM

PRESENTED BY
SDM MAGAZINE ✳ GETT PLUGGED ENT. ✳ TEAM MONEY HUNGRY

# BET★ HONOR AWARDS

## AUG 19

**5401 CASS AVE | DETROIT, MI 48202 | 7PM - 10PM**

Hosted by
Precious Houston

Co-Hosted
by Bino

# SDM

**EDITOR-IN-CHIEF**
D. "Casino" Bailey
casino@sdmlive.com

**EDITORIAL DIRECTOR**
Sheree Cranford
sheree@sdmlive.com

**GRAPHIC/WEB DESIGNER**
D. "Casino" Bailey
casino@sdmlive.com

**A&R MANAGER**
Aye Money
ayemoney@sdmlive.com

**ACCOUNT EXECUTIVE**
Frank Harvest Jr.
frank@sdmlive.com

**PHOTOGRAPHERS**
Treagen Colston
D. "Casino" Bailey

**CONTRIBUTORS**
April Smiley
Courtney Benjamin

**COPY ORDERS & ADVERTISING OFFICE**
**Send Money Order or Check to:**
Mocy Publishing
P.O. Box 35195
Detroit, Michigan 48235
(586) 646-8505
advertise@sdmlive.com

**Copy Order Item #:**
SDM Magazine Issue #9 2016
S&H Plus Retail Price - $9.99 per copy

**WWW.SDMLIVE.COM**

**Printed by CreateSpace, An Amazon.com Company**

## MP
MOCY PUBLISHING

Copyright © 2016 Support Detroit Movement,
a division of Aye Money Promotions & Publishing, LLC and
Mocy Music Publishing, LLC. All rights reserved.
Printed in the U.S.A.

REAL MUSIC. REAL ENTERTAINMENT.

# SDM

ISSUE 9

ALSO
SHAWNTA MCDOUGLE
KYLE GREENLAW
ROSE MCCROY
CIENTELL
PLUS MORE

QUENTIN SHARPE
BRANDING HIMSELF
WITH ACTING SKILLS

GUCCI RIE
PERSUING HER
DREAMS AS
AN ACTRESS

STARRING
KIMBERLY "BURNADEBT" KANE
THE HOTTEST MAMA AROUND...

# BURNING IT DOWN

THE CAST OF MARK HUNTER'S STAGE PLAY
"LET IT BURN" HAS TAKEN OVER THE SDM
MAGAZINE THIS MONTH

# CONTENTS

**1**

**Insignia™ - 39" Class (38.5" Diag.) - LED - 1080p - Smart - HDTV Roku TV - Black**
$249.99
www.bestbuy.com

**2**

**Microsoft - Xbox One S 2TB Console**
$399.99
www.bestbuy.com

**3**

**LG - Ultra Slim 8x Max. DVD Write Speed External USB DVD±RW/CD-RW Drive - Black**
$29.99
www.bestbuy.com

# Black Lives Face White Supremacy

## STORIES FLOOD THE NATION WITH WHITE LAW OFFICIALS WRONGFULLY ABUSING THEIR POSITIONS OF POWER TO KILL THE BLACK RACE.

by Cheraee C.

America is shifting into a place where all you need is to be a white man with a badge to be licensed to kill. The white on black war has been going on for centuries and every since the cold death of Trayvon Martin in 2012, it seems like white cops in America have been apart of a domino effect. George Zimmerman got away with murder and every cop that has took a black life seems to be easily acquitted from murder also as they use their badge, the victim's past, and unnecessary police tactics to defend themselves.

Society is in a heap of confusion because if a man, any man, any color, any class, any career kills another being, nothing should limit them from the community frowning upon them and disowning them as a murderer. Nothing should excuse them from the death penalty, life in prison without parole, or any consequence or lawful punishment. Clearly cops need to re-evaluate the men they are making cops and the manipulative ways they are training these cops. Now the legal system is flawed from the judges to the way hard evidence is perceived. Now the way we define justice is flawed, and now our freedom is flawed. How can we believe in justice if it's never served when cases and trials are lost that should've been won? How can we be free if we can killed by a cop just for upholding the law and pulling over at a traffic stop?

It's 2016 and here we are again with the current murders of Alton Sterling and Philando Castille. Two innocent black men in two different states who police brutally murdered. White men fear the black race as a threat to them, which we are. We have a black president, black billionaires, black entrepreneurs, black businesses, and we need to start embracing our blackness. Tomorrow is not promised to us which is why we need to stop fighting the wrong battles and making enemies. In America, America's Most Wanted is becoming obsolete because white cops are becoming public enemy number one.

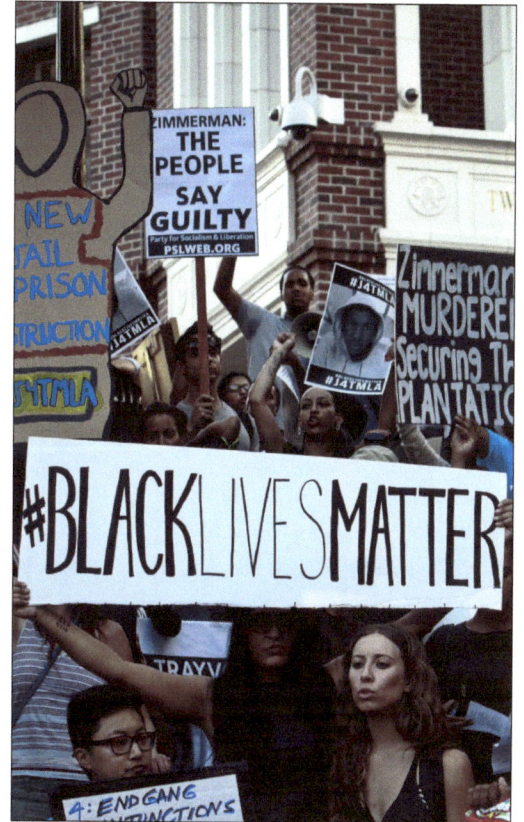

# The Scarface Saga Returns

AUTHOR STANLEY L. BATTLE RETURNS WITH SCARFACE 2 WITH A PLOT OF EMOTIONAL AND CRIMINAL INTENSITY.

**by Cheraee C.**

Antonio Montero's son was young and feeble in Scarface Part 1, but in this grimey continuation it breaks down his stepfather's (Shawn Bomosk) downfall, and his godfather's (Alvin Stone) uprising, as Antonio experiences loss, racism, and matures into a wealthy man of power.

After graduating high school with a Porsche, Antonio decides that he wants to be apart of the infamous drug cartel hailing from Columbia led by Sorcerer. If only Antonio knew the true identity and cold realities of the man he was trapping for, he probably would've picked another career and went to college. Only time, Antonio's darkest times will reveal to him the naked truth. Will Antonio survive a mind of revenge, countless enemies, and a great state of depression?

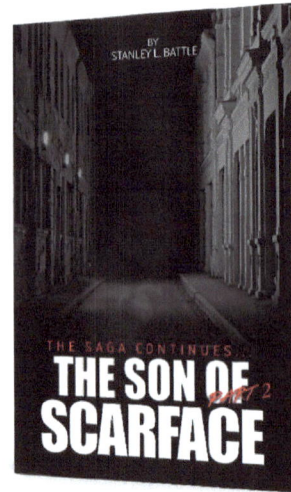

**Scarface Part 2**
*By Stanley L. Battle*

*Available from Amazon.com and other online stores*

# M

## VIDEOS
## TOP 20
## EVERYDAY
## 10AM 6PM 2AM

SDM on Roku TV

# Ms. Burnadebt Shuts It Down

KIMBERLY KANE PLAYS THE LEAD ROLE MS. BURNADEBT AS A SINCERE, HIGHLY-CONFIDENT, AND LOYAL WOMAN LIVING LIFE TO THE FULLEST.
by Cheraee C.

Q. How did you meet Mark Hunter and what role do you play in Let It Burn?

A. Interesting that you ask... I met Mark Hunter in January of 2014 when I went to audition for a Shoe Lady Productions play that he co-wrote. The play was called Stay In Your Place, and I read opposite Mark for the role (Sandra) that I subsequently landed in that play, and later went on to keep that same role in Stay In Your Place the movie. A friend recommended that I audition for Let It Burn. I orginially read for the part of Pearl, and that was the role I landed... until the first table read. At the first table read EVERYONE'S roles changed, and I ended up with the lead role Ms. Burnadebt.

Q. Let It Burn went from Detroit to Alabama in five months. Did you expect Let It Burn to go national so quickly, and what are your thoughts about the wave this play has created?

A. I LOVE it! After reading the script, and then interacting with the cast, and our director Shawnta McDougle, I had a pretty good idea that the play would be very successful! I am very much excited about the wave that the play has created. Each and every cast member has worked hard and tirelessly to bring our best performances to the stage in hopes to entertain our audience, and leave a lasting smile and wonderful memories from the "Let It Burn" experience.

Q. Does your character Ms. Burnadebt remind you of yourself in any ways, and what is your favorite scene with Ms. Burnadebt?

A. Yes, Ms. Burnadebt reminds me of myself in many ways. I am fiercely protective of my family. I have a huge sense of humor, and I believe in keeping it 100% REAL. My favorite Ms. Burnadebt scene is the scene where Ms. Burnadebt introduces her ex-husband's which leads to the most hysterically funny scene between Pearl and Burnadebt!

Q. Do you know any of your castmates personally and have you acted with any of your castmates in other productions?

A. Rose McCroy and I hit it off a few years ago at an audition, but hadn't seen each other since. During the audition, somehow we just KNEW we would be Burnadebt and Pearl because of our chemistry! I was so glad to finally work with her! I didn't know any of my other castmates "personally." I had seen some of them in other productions, but the personal interactions didn't happen until Let It Burn, and NOW we are all friends!

# Mr. Funny Kyle Greenlaw

KYLE GREENLAW'S PLAYS AS A JANITOR IN THE STAGE PLAY "LET IT BURN"
AND HE BRINGS THE HOUSE DOWN WITH HIS FUNNY CHARACTER.

**by Cheraee C.**

**Q. How did you and Mark Hunter cross paths and what role do you play in Let It Burn?**

A. Mark and I met where deals in the hood are made… THE BARBERSHOP! He and I have the same barber, Mr. Brian Reeve's proprietor, Change Barbershop. Mark was looking for an older cat for a role in his stage play "Man Up" and B spoke on me. The rest is history! I'm currently playing the role of "Otis the custodian" in Let It Burn.

**Q. What struck your interest in theatre and what are some of the things you have learned from all the productions you have been in?**

A. I'm driven! Theatre allows me the distinct pleasure of using acting as another vehicle/source to have a voice and present the very best of me! Being in theatre, I've learned the art of digging deeper into myself to become the character, further learning more about myself and my ability, and focus for a successful outcome. I practice and rehearse my lines at work with the automation of robotics as my audience, talking out loud to myself, and having folk look at me cock-eyed thinking I'm crazy living the part off stage!

**Q. Playing a janitor or an old man role is cool, but if you could play any role in theatre, what would it be and why?**

A. Wow… I'm very open to any role certainly to sharpen my talent and broaden its potential. However, the role of a pastor is always so near and dear to my heart. But, I think I'd play the hell out of the role of being the father of "Cookie" on Empire…lol…ijs! Oh…you did say "theatre"! I'd play a judge, pastor, or politician; if only I could sing…

**Q. You plan to keep rolling with Let It Burn across the nation and are you taking on other productions at the same time?**

A. Yes, I'm rolling with Let It Burn across the nation and I am open and expecting greater work to come even while touring with the FABOLOUS production.

# Rose McCroy as Ms. Pearl

MS. PEARL IS MS. BURNADEBT'S BEST FRIEND WHO IS A WOMAN WITH LAYERS OF HURT AND FEAR THAT SHE MASKS THROUGH THE USE OF THE BIBLE.

**by Cheraee C.**

Q. How did you meet Mark Hunter and how did you become apart of the Let It Burn cast?
A. Mark had came to several shows I was in and we were also FB friends... I reached out to him after his auditions for Let It Burn and he asked me to come to his first table read. I landed a role that day!

Q. What chaacter do you play in Let it Burn and what do you like most about your role?
A. I play the character of Ms. Pearl. What I like most about the character is the fact that she has kinda like 2 sides to her. She used to be in the streets, but now she is saved. Sometimes she likes to go back to her old ways with her best friend Burnadebt secretly. So with that being said, it makes me as an actress stretch myself.

Q. What or who inspired you to become an actress and what waere the first small and major acting gigs you did?
A. What inspired me was my very first show, which was a small production at my old church. The show was very different. The characters on stage performed the actions as me, myself, and other castmates delivered the lines behind the scene. I played two characters. The response I got from the audience at the end was wonderful! They never knew that I was speaking two different characters. That was really the first show, however my first major show/role was "Just For the Love of Money" with Finn Productions.

Q. What are some things in your life that you've had to let go and let burn?
A. If I can be a little transparent right now, i have had to cut ties with people that did not have my best interest at heart. Severing ties of long relationships are not easy, but sometimes necessary. if you want to continue to gorw. I took a leap and stepped out on faith alone with a goal of being my own boss! So, my 9-5 is Let it Burn! However, I am forever grateful for all it has taught me over the years.

Q. Seeing that acting is your career, tell us what other steps have you taken to invest more into your career?

A. So far I've taken several acting classes with different directors here in Metro Detroit. Classes such as characteer breakdown, determining the backstory of the character, the study of scenes, amongst other development training. I've most recently enrolled in Schoolcraft College Theatre Program. My goal here would allow me to enhance on a whole other arena. The course will end with me holding a degree in theatre as well as being well-prepared to move forward in my career. I'm even more confident with all the projects I've worked on, my goal is to learn and advance from each production, learning something new from the writer, diector/producer, as well as my other castmates. The take away from each project helps me to develop and evolve as an actress.

# The Spectacular City Girl Neka

GUCCI RIE PLAYS A YOUNG, CLUELESS, HUMOROUS FEMALE HUSTLA NAMED NEKA WHO GOT THEM BUNDLES ON DECK.

**by Cheraee C.**

**Q. How did you meet Mark Hunter and what role do you play in Let It Burn?**

A. I saw Mark Hunter's casting call online so I screenshotted it and got prepared to go to the auditions. I wasn't sure if I won them over because I never got a call back. So I saw him post again for a second audition looking for a female actress. I inboxed him again with some headshots of me and told him to give me a try I will be REMARKABLE. He told me to come in for the second audition. I don't think I did my best because he felt it was a better actress in the room with me who nailed the part better so I left feeling sad. That's when Mark came running out to me and said hold on i got the perfect part for you... I knew that was GOD'S FAVOR and I was chosen... I told him I promise you got yourself a winer. That's how I met Mark Hunter. I play the role of NEKA, love her, she got them bundles on deck... very funny girl in the play. A little spacey, but I can handle it lol. Fir.st, I was like not so sure because I wanted a bigger role, but after so many rehearsals I knew I was NEKA... LOVE NEKA.. She is your everyday city girl or should I say sexy thot lol swinghair... well I'm an actress... play your role diva!

**Q. With the new members that have been added to the cast to hit Alabama, who are you most excited about working with and why?**

A. I'm super excited about going to Alabama; this will be good to have this under my belt being a new actress. Bigger stage, bigger crowd, yes! And it's a beauty! I'm so excited to be sharing the stage with CELEBRITY Willie Taylor from Love And Hip Hop Hollywood. First off I was a fan from when he was singing in Day 26. Besides, he so fine lol cool guy, madd talented, and I must say all the other cast members we are family... love them all! We all stars! Let It Burn!

**Q. What's the next acting gig you plan to venture off on and what's next for Let It Burn?**

A. Maybe with Sheree in the future in her web series and we taking Let It Burn to Chicago and Dallas... It's about to get busy, but my eyes is open to some new opportunities! I totally believe they coming soon... I'm READY, ready for the Big Screen, Big Stage, Big Checks!

# Staying Connected To The Streets

LEEK HUSTLE TALKS ABOUT HIS INTRODUCTION TO MUSIC AND HOW HE PLANS TO NOT BE LABELED AS ONE GENRE OF RAP.

**by Cheraee C.**

**Q.** Leek, you have worked with a lot of heavy hitters so how did you manage to make those musical connections?

A. I make the connections I make by establishing good, working relationships, being 100 with people, and staying bout my business with good vibes.

**Q.** What were the first internet markets you put your music on, what music did you feature, and in your opinion what is the most beneficial internet market for music of your caliber?

A. Dat Piff and YouTube were the first internet markets I used. I put my first album I ever did Realism Chapter 1 on them which is still available and features some good songs. YouTube is the best because it's easier for people to find music and I feel like people are visual. YouTube also brings music to life about

**Q.** Do you consider yourself to be a universal rapper who will rap to any genre or are you just strictly trap music?

A. No not at all... Lol it all depends on my emotions; music talks to me. I think once people hear Trap Love my new mixtape, the view of trap rapper will change to me being just an artist.

**Q.** So you feel like most people view you as a trap rapper and that's kind of an understatement because you rather be viewed as simply an artist with levels?

A. I think that some view me as just that... But I feel once they hear Trap Love some other layers of my music will be revealed. I am very versatile. You will see once Trap Love drops.

**Q.** Tell us three things about yourself that takes us beyond music, that people don't know, but would like to know.

A. I have a son and he is my world and my motivation to do better. I was raised in a shelter by my moms with my brothers, and I really enjoy listening to old school music like The Whispers, Teddy, and the Ohio Players.

**Q.** If I was to interview you six months from now, what do you think would be different/new in your music career?

A. Six months from now I would be touring around the United States finishing up my next project called Hustle Man. We would be talking most definitely, more about 100 Music Group as a growing staple in the music industry. BASICALLY the next wave taking what God sends me. I got a team of real spittas... 100 MG mixtape with just my crew cooking. But Trapping For Real is the single out on my mixtapes; download that app and download Leek Hustle Trapping For Real and look for Trap Love coming out soon, thank you, and God bless.

# Apple's U.S. Nuisance

## STREAMING COMPETITION IS HEATING UP AS SPOTIFY REVENUES SKY ROCKET.

**by** Semaja Turner

Who would've ever thought that Apple, one of America's wealthiest technology companies with over 478 Apple retail stores worldwide would be under the government's microscope? Apparently, Apple is under investigation by the federal government for doing some unjust musical practices. Apple hasn't being playing fair with its streaming company competitors and everybody's complaining especially Spotify. Rivals like Spotify are saying that Apple wants to have its cake and eat it too because Apple is reportedly making more money off of a Spotify subscription then it is off of an Apple Music subscription, and not sharing any of the profits.

The fact of the matter is Apple created its app store with its own funds, so why can't the company charge others for the right to be in their app store? And why is the federal government so concerned with Apple? Shouldn't it be more concerned about the upcoming presidency and all the police killings around America instead of picking on billion dollar companies? Currently, it hasn't been decided if the U.S. is going to pursue a lawsuit against Apple or not, but Apple better start brainstorming of ways to get back on the federal government's good side because Google, Amazon, and Spotify is not having its foolery.

# Up and Coming Actor Q-Heffner

## QUE IS BECOMING THE KING OF BRANDING AS A HOST AND PROMOTER WITH A RADIO SHOW, A BOW TIE LINE, AND ACTING ROLES ON THE WAY!

**by Cheraee C.**

**Describe how you met Mark Hunter and how you become a part of the Let It Burn production?**

I met Mark Hunter from a mutual friend we have DJ Hi-Lyte that connected us on a party I'm a party promoter and a host, Q-Heffner Ent. He saw how I vibe with the crowd and my personality and my attire. And after the event Mark and I kicked it for like two hours and he was like I have a roll that's perfect for you. It's basically you playing you lol… so a few months went by and he kept his word. He called me and I went to the auditions and it was on from their.

**Describe the character you play in Let It Burn and what you enjoy most about your role?**

I play the role of Devin Mays's slick talking, well-dressed businessman who's taken over his father's business. He sweet talks Sheryl Johnson who is a successful business-woman who's taking over her father's business and is falling head over heels for me. The whole time I'm really out to get her money while her mother Ms. Burnadebt is on to my scheme lol and what they do to me at the end wow… can't give it away. You have to come out and see the play "Let It Burn" it's a roller coaster ride. You'll laugh, cry, and cheer.

**How long have you been acting or is this your first acting gig?**

I did a small movie roll prior to this, but actually this is my first roll. Mark saw something in me that I knew was there, but hadn't tapped into yet… but now he created a monster lol. I have like four acting rolls since Let It Burn.

**So what four acting roles have you gotten since Let It Burn? I'm in a few independent movies called "Tru Religion" and "Have You Seen Shorty?"**

I'm in a stage play due out in October opening in Atlanta of this year called "I Am What God Says I Am." I'm also in a movie called "Heavy Hustle." Let It Burn has been a great opportunity. The cast of Let It Burn, we're family. We support each other's ventures outside of Let It Burn. We really respect each other. I thank God, my family, Detroit city, and my dude Mark Hunter. All these people are rooting for me. Look out for me, I'm up and coming from Q-Heffner Ent. My radio show coming out Q-Heffner Show and my bow tie line Quen Sharpe Collection (QSC.) When you have Detroit with you, man you can make it anywhere and trust me the city is with me. Quentin Sharpe, Q- Heffner Ent.

**How do you feel about Let It Burn going on tour around the world and working alongside Willie Taylor and Tameka Scott?**

Let It Burn going on tour is crazy… I'm excited, nervous, and anxious all in one. I'm really excited to represent Southwest Detroit and the Westside of Detroit where I was raised and developed. Detroit as a whole.. the city is filled with talent going on tour is a blessing I appreciate every minute of it. Being alongside Willie Taylor is big; you build relationships. I met him years ago with Day 26 in a Detroit night club. It will make me step my game up and Tameka Scott, I've always been a fan of Xscape. I play their music to this day so being alongside of her will be an honor. I'm like a sponge; I'm a question them to death about the game and pick their brain.

# Director Shawnta McDougle

## DIRECTING AN ALLSTAR CAST MRS. SHAWNTA MCDOUGLE IS ON A MISSION TO BECOME DETROIT'S NEXT TOP DIRECTOR AND ACTING COACH.

**by Cheraee C.**

**Q. How did you meet Mark Hunter and how did you end up directing Let It Burn?**

A. Ok… I met Mark through an actress I was teaching and directing on a project. She told me that he was a good guy and that he could use a director like me. She gave him my information and he contacted me and the rest is history. We vibed from the very beginning; he told me what he was trying to do and I was interested in what he was trying to do in theatre. I'm a teacher by heart and I love instructing and directing actors who are hungry for work; those who have talent, but know they need training.

**Q. Besides working with Mark Hunter, who are some other upcoming people in theatre that you've worked with and what led you to work with them?**

A. After graduating from Albany State University with a BA in Speech and Theatre, trained by A.C. Myles, I was blessed to work with Gary Anderson, Robert Douglas, Reuben Yabuku, and D.lrean. They have been staples in the Detroit and national theater community.

**Q. Describe exactly how Gary Anderson, Robert Douglas, Reuben Yabuku, and D.lrean are staples in the Detroit theater community?**

A. Gary Anderson of Plowshares Theatre Company years ago gave me an internship with his company. I believe they are the only professional black theatre company in Detroit. He and his company were very helpful to me when I was searching for direction as a newbie to the theatre world. Reuben of Buku Production has been in this community for many years. He directed me in wake up and face reality which was a small theater production. I attended his acting class one and two. He has directed National touring shows in the United States. Robert Douglas is a hands-on educator of theatre. He is my go-to when I'm not sure about thing. D.lrean is an awesome Christian writer/director.

**Q. Other then Let It Burn, have any of the other productions you've directed went national and if so what cities did the productions travel too?**

A. Oh no, not yet. I love small beginnings!

**Q. So Let It Burn is the first production for you that went international?**

A. First nationally toured play yes.

**Q. What city in the United States whether booked or not booked for the tour would you like to see Let It Burn hit the stage of?**

A. I would love to see Let It Burn reboot in Detroit again and then tour to Chicago and Dallas and beyond…

**Q. What's your favorite role in the Let It Burn production and why?**

A. All the characters are very good roles and written well, however, Ms. Burnadebt is my favorite! She says things that many want to say, but don't have the nerves to say. She is off kilter on some of her philosophies, however her heart is good. She is spunky, crazy, energetic, and even soft at times, but genuine. And Kimberly (Pinctoes) Kane totally brings her to life!

**Q. Detroit has been becoming a hotspot for theatre and film. What is your opinion of Detroit its growing entertainment sector in terms of film/theatre?**

A. Detroit is full of talented people. I know many actors who just need opportunities to train and work. Many are humble and desire to grown. I think this city is big enough for theatre and film at the same time.

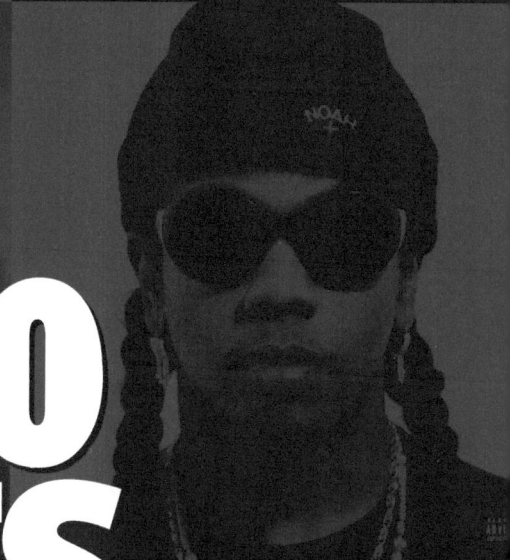

# TOP 10 CHARTS

## TOP 10 DIGITAL SINGLES AND ALBUMS
### JULY 1, 2016

# TOP 10 CHARTS

## TOP #1

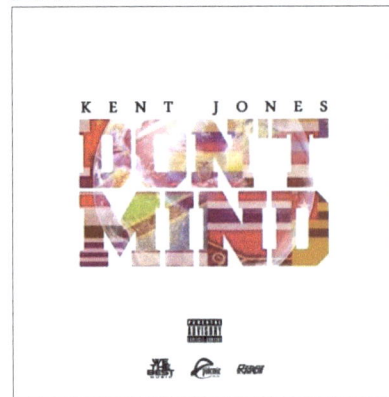

### Kent Jones
*Don't Mind*

*Coming in at #1 this month, Kent has everybody grooving and dnacing to his jam.*

## TOP 10 SINGLES CHART OF THE MONTH

| No. | Artist - Song Title |
|-----|---------------------|
| 1 | KENT JONES - DON'T MIND |
| 2 | FUTURE - WICKED |
| 3 | MADEINTYO - UBER EVYERWHERE |
| 4 | FAT JOE/REMY MA - ALL THE WAY UP |
| 5 | DRAKE - CONTROLLA |
| 6 | TI/MARSHA AMBROSIUS - DOPE |
| 7 | DJ KHALED/DRAKE - FOR FREE |
| 8 | 50 CENT/CHRIS BROWN - I'M THE MAN ( REMIX) |
| 9 | MOBDIVA - IS YOU ROLLIN |
| 10 | WALE - MY PYT |

## TOP 10 ALBUMS CHART OF THE MONTH

| No. | Artist - Album Title |
|-----|----------------------|
| 1 | YG - STILL BRASY |
| 2 | SNOOP DOGG - COOLAID |
| 3 | CHRISETTE MICHELE - MILESTONE |
| 4 | BRYSON TILLER - TRAPSOUL |
| 5 | RO JAMES - ELDORADO |
| 6 | KANYE WEST - THE LIFE OF PABLO |
| 7 | KEVIN GATES - ISLAH |
| 8 | OT GENASIS - RHYTHM & BRICKS |
| 9 | USHER - FLAWED |
| 10 | KING DILLON - THE CORONATION |

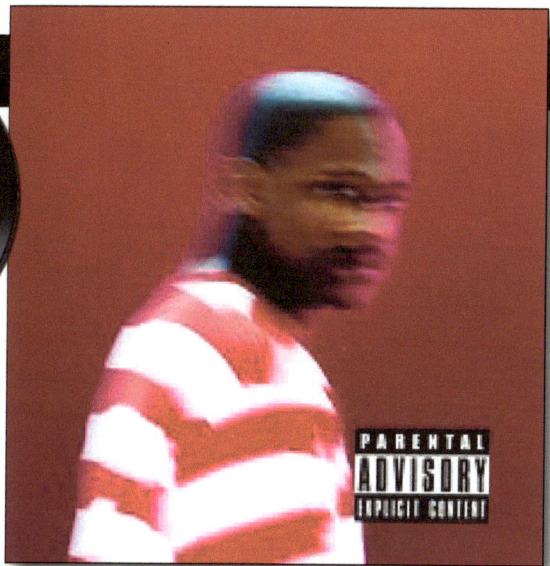

## Still Brazy

**ARTIST:** YG
**REVIEWER:** Cheraee C.
**RATING:** 4

Usually rapper YG is flowing about racks and his hittas, but in this notable album he's expressing his views on race, the police, and police brutality in America. Tracks include Police Get Away Wit Murder, Blacks and Browns featuring Sad Boy, Nothing Wrong featuring The Game, Ice Cube, and Snoop Dogg, I Got a Question featuring Lil Wayne, Ice Kold Killas featuring Ice Cube, Bool, Balm, and Collective, and many other tracks. I give this album four stars.

**RATE METER:  1 - WACK  2 - NEEDS WORK  3 - STRAIGHT  4 - BANGER  5 - CLASSIC**

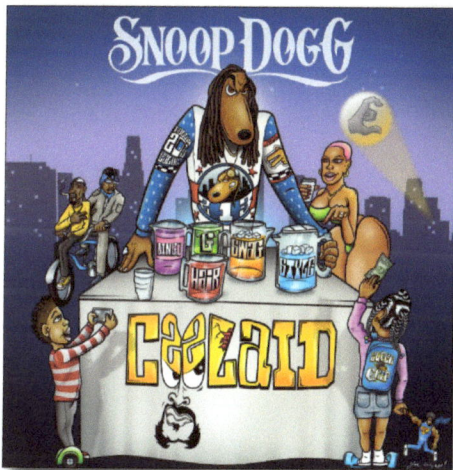

## Coolaid

**ARTIST:** Snoop Dogg
**REVIEWER:** Cheraee C.
**RATING:** 4

The OG Snoop Dogg returns with another smooth, classic album with all the greats. Tracks on this mixtape include Let the Beat Drop (Celebrate) featuring Swizz Beatz, Kush Ups featuring Wiz Khalifa, Double Tap featuring E-40 and Jazze Pha, Affliated featuring Trick Trick, Don't Know featuring Too Short, and many other tracks. I give this album four stars.

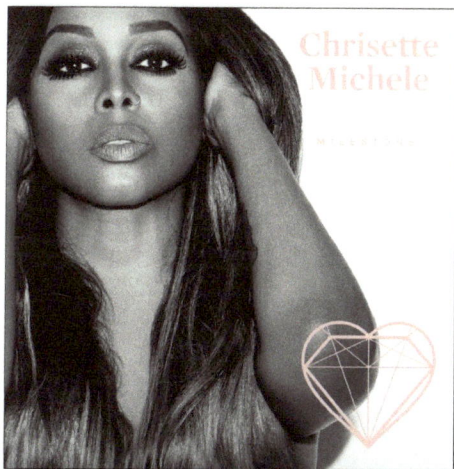

## Milestone

**ARTIST:** Chrisette Michele
**REVIEWER:** Cheraee C.
**RATING:** 3

Chrisette Michele is a very eccentric artist with a rare style. Some of her music is very dope while the rest of her music is uncategorized, but like she says she's not that just one sound. Tracks from this album include Steady, Soulmate, Indy Girl, Reinvent the Wheel. and Us Against the World. i give her album four stars.

# HEELS & SKILLZ

## Cristina Cold
is a full-time model from Detroit, MI.

**instagram**
@cristinacold2

*Photography by*
*@barearmy*

# HEELS &
# SKILLZ

**Faren**

is a beautiful model
from Orlando, FL.

**instagram**
@missfarenw

*Photography by*
*@barearmy*

# HEELS & SKILLZ

**Lisa Bella**

is a sexy model
for barearmy and
lives in Waterford, MI.

**facebook**
lisabella

# Cheraee's Corner

## WHY DON'T BLACK PEOPLE SUPPORT OTHER BLACK PEOPLE?

**by Cheraee C.**

There is no reason why black people shouldn't support other black people, but we live in a society where there's black on black crime every day. Not only are we at war with our own race, but we are at war with our own flesh and blood. Some of us despise the color of our own skin so much that we try to bleach our skin light and white like it's not an honor to be black. Black people are warriors and survivors who have succumbed to some of the greatest challenges in history yet we have no ambition to support one another. Black people have internalized black power wrong and have brain-washed ourselves into being bitter, selfish, envious, and competitive individuals.

Instead of black people honoring each other like we are taught too, we become adults and become so arrogant that we ignore our fundamentals. Somehow the genuine spirit of compassion has come and gone like the wind because we let pain, heart-ache, misery, materialistic items, and gossip dictate us. Everybody is aiming for the number one spot, as if we all can't have a number one spot. We are all winners and achievers, and if we supported each other like we should it would be more black businesses, stronger black businesses, and the black community would be a stronger entity.

The lack of support is what causes the fury in black people because we let our opinions and perceptions of black people build bridges. Let's start bridging the gap with positive energy and supportive vibes despite our personal feelings or differences.

# NEXT 2 BLOW

## MAK LOO

**Q.** Who is Mak Loo and how has the music industry changed since you got started?

A. I'm a man with a vision and a grind that wants to help my people be better people. The music industry changed from being authentic to glorifying money instead of message and the talent... S/O to J.Cole.

**Q.** In a field where a rapper is being born everyday, what would you say are your strengths and weaknesses?

A. My strengths is being real and just being me. A lot of deez niggas make up shyt. I just stay real and real niggaz know the difference when they see it and when they hear it.

**Q.** When do you have time to incorporate music into your daily schedule and what's a day in your life consist of?

A. My daily life consists of me spending time with my son, working a job, and just staying out da way. I incorporate music in between raising my son and working a job because it's a time for everything.

**Q.** What would you say is the biggest accomplishment you've made so far in the industry?

A. Having random people I don't know, knowing my lyrics and appreciating my music.

Q. According to social media you are the crreater of Cien-City so what exactly is Cien-City and what made you create it?

A. CienCity (pronounced) Sin-City is a prefix of my first name and City represents my world of music, dance, and fashion.

Q. As an artist what level do you feel like you've reached in the music world?

A. I most definitely have a long way to go in my career. It's like I'm still in the beginning stages. There's more demographics and countries to reach. I'm just getting started.

Q. Besides the joy of music, you are currently expecting. How is your new addition affecting your music career?

A. My bundle of joy is motivation for me to keep pursuing my dreams, you know? It's giving me more inspiration to write and I believe I can reach the world by writing music about motherhood.

Q. Do you plan to go back to music full throttle after the birth of your baby?

A. Yes I most definitely plan to go full throttle back in the studio after the baby's born. I've been spending time writing music and resting my mind, body, and soul.

Q. Since you are a songwriter can you freestyle a few lyrics for us and show the world how Cien flow...

A. Oh my goodness! I was just writing a few lines about my baby, but here's what I got for now haha! What makes me happy is feeling your love in my belly, life forming in my womb, that's true wealth to me, all the money in the world doesn't ammount up to how complete I am, how complete I am.

Q. Tell us how you found out about SDM Magazine and how it feels to have a certified interview?

A. I found out about SDM mag from seeing trap R&B Neisha Neshae on the cover and I love the outline of the mag too! Some of my favorite artists have been featured like Holly Monrahh. It's such a honor to be featured in the mag!

*CIENTELL*

# SNAP SHOTS

**Email Your Snap Shots to**
snapshots@sdmlive.com

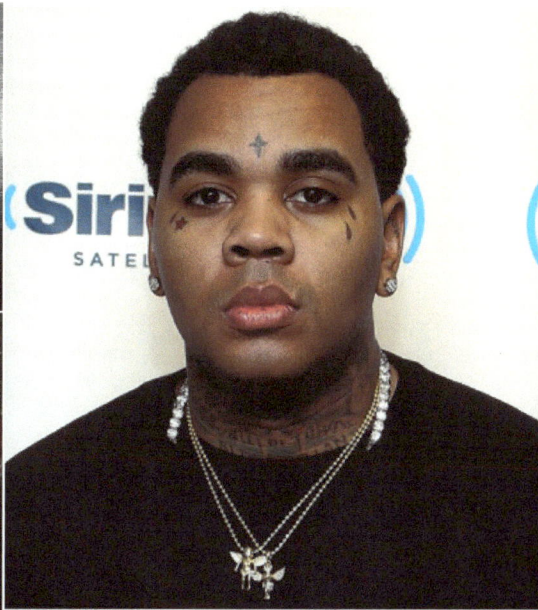

#BLACK LIVES MATTER

IS MY SON NEXT?

# 5DS PRODUCTIONS®
### THE PRINT MEDIA CENTER.

# PRINT

## GET 10% OFF WITH CODE: SAVE10OFF

## DIGITAL & PRESS RUN PRICE LIST

**BUSINESS CARD**
2x3.5 INCHES

| | |
|---|---|
| 100 | $10 |
| 500 | $20 |
| 1000 | $30 |
| 5000 | $100 |
| 10000 | $170 |

**TRIFOLD BROCHURE**
8.5x11 INCHES

| | |
|---|---|
| 250 | $150 |
| 500 | $180 |
| 1000 | $230 |
| 5000 | $350 |
| 10000 | $680 |

**POSTCARDS**
4x6 INCHES

| | |
|---|---|
| 250 | $50 |
| 500 | $55 |
| 1000 | $65 |
| 5000 | $130 |
| 10000 | $250 |

FLYERS - BROCHURES - BANNERS - BUSINESS CARDS - CD INSERTS
CALENDARS - EVENT TICKETS - POSTCARDS - POSTERS
YARD SIGNS - AND MUCH MORE

DIGITAL & PRESS RUN PRINTING

FAST TURN AROUND PRINTING

GET FREE SHIPPING ON ALL ORDERS

## YOU SAVE MONEY WHEN YOU PRINT AT
# WWW.THEPRINTMEDIACENTER.COM
## 24/7 ONLINE ORDERING. CALL US NOW 1.888.718.2999

COUPON CODE IS FOR A LIMITED TIME OFFER - FREE UPS SHIPPING ANYWHERE IN THE US

# Urban Fiction, Spiritual, Motivation and more.
## Order a book from Mocy Publishing today and receive FREE shipping.

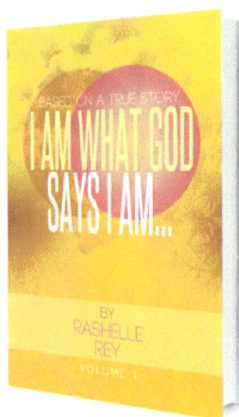

**I Am What God Says I Am...**
*By Rashelle Rey*

Item #: IAWGS29
Price: $9.99

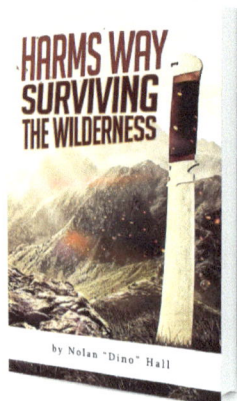

**Harm's Way**
*By Nolan "Dino" Hall*

Item #: HWS821
Price: $15.99

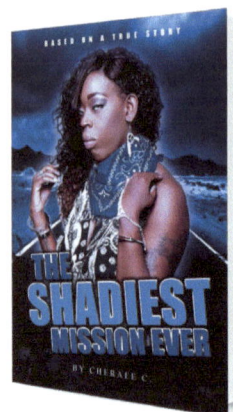

**The Shadiest Mission Ever**
*By Cheraee C.*

Item #: TSME28
Price: $12.99

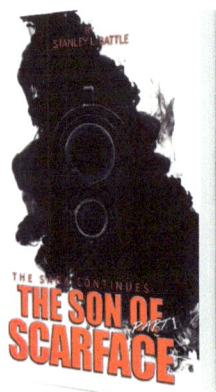

**The Son Of Scarface – Part 1**
*By Stanley L. Battle*

Item #: TSOS01
Price: $12.99

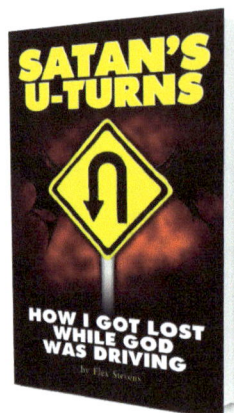

**Satan's U-Turns**
*By Flex Stevens*

Item #: SUT382
Price: $9.99

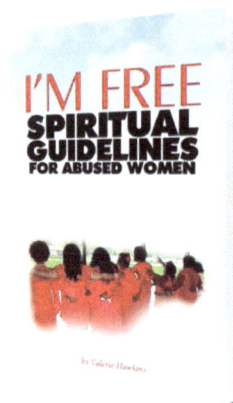

**I'm Free**
*By Valerie Hawkins*

Item #: IFTSG82
Price: $14.99

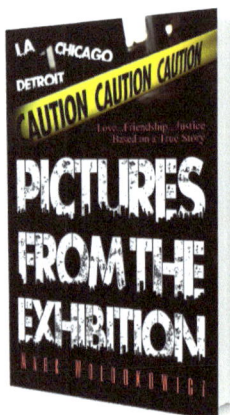

**Pictures From The Exhibition**
*By Mark Wolodkowicz*

Item #: PFAE292
Price: $15.99

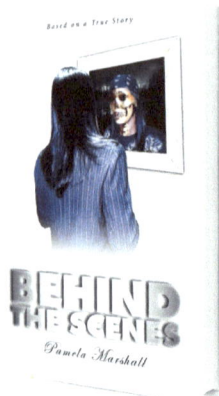

**Behind The Scenes**
*By Pamela Marshall*

Item #: BTS721
Price: $15.99

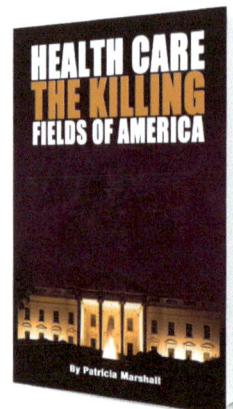

**Health Care**
*By Patricia Marshall*

Item #: HCTABF2
Price: $17.99

# www.mocypublishing.com
## order online and receive FREE shipping. Limit time offer.

# LOOKING FOR A NEW LOOK

## LET US CREATE A NEW WEBSITE FOR YOUR COMPANY FOR LESS.

## Basic

### $3.99/month

1 Website
10 GB Storage
25,000 Monthly Vistors

### PLUS

\* FREE Monthly Hosting

\* Get a FREE Domain with annual plan

## Standard

### $4.99/month

1 Website
15 GB Storage
100,000 Monthly Vistors

### PLUS

\* FREE Monthly Hosting

\* Search engine optimization plugin

\* Get a FREE Domain with annual plan

## Premium

### $12.99/month

1 Website
50 GB Storage
800,000 Monthly Vistors

### PLUS

\* FREE Monthly Hosting

\* Search engine optimization plugin

\* RapidSSL Certificate

\* Get a FREE Domain with annual plan

We offer complete WordPress website design and development. From a simple website to an advanced business e-Commerce solution, we can create the ultimate solution to meet your marketing goals and objectives.

All of our custom website builds follow a structured development process which helps us execute your project on-time and on-budget. For prices go to www.5DShost.com/websites

# 5DSHOST
## THE BEST FOR HOSTING

Call Our Support:
# (888) 718-2999
## WWW.5DSHOST.COM

REAL MUSIC. REAL ENTERTAINMENT.

# S.DM

ISSUE 3

ALSO
**AUHMAZ!N**
**ISHMAELSOUL**
**MZ. PLATINUM**
**KID JAY**

## KOSTA
JUST HIT THE JACKPOT WITH A NEW SMASH HIT SINGLE "LOTTERY"

## BIGG DAWG BLAST
LAUNCHES THE STREET HITTA DJ'S MOVEMENT

# Neisha Neshae

BRINGING IN 2016 ON STAGE WITH THE KING OF R&B R-KELLY & DROPPING A NEW MIXTAPE

PLUS MORE

## THE RED CARPET EDITION
SUPERSTARS CAME WITH FASHION AT THE SDM MAGAZINE RELEASE PARTY

US - $9.99  CANADA - $14.99

01 >

9 770317 847001

JANUARY 2016 No.3
WWW.SDMLIVE.COM

*THE ALL NEW STYLE OF MAGAZINE-BOOKS*

**For advertisement**
please call (586) 646-8505
or visit www.sdmlive.com

www.ingramcontent.com/pod-product-compliance
Lightning Source LLC
Chambersburg PA
CBHW040019050426
42452CB00002B/45